THE

FORMULA

VOL. 2

GAME CHANGING STRATEGIES
FROM EVERYDAY EXPERTS

THE

FORMULA

VOL. 2

GAME CHANGING STRATEGIES
FROM EVERYDAY EXPERTS

JAI STONE

THE FORMULA, VOL. 2
Published by The Brand Coach

Copyright © 2019 Jai Stone

Printed in the United States of America
ISBN: 978-0-578-45263-0

DOWNLOAD YOUR GIFT!
FREE BADASS BRAND BLUEPRINT

READ THIS FIRST

Thank you for purchasing my book!
As a token of my appreciation, I'd like to give you the
companion profit system at NO COST.

DOWNLOAD YOUR GIFT AT:

www.jaistone.com/badass

Join My
ONLINE COMMUNITY

The Brand & Hustle with Jai Stone community is where highly driven, serious women entrepreneur Game ChangHERs come to learn, build your business, your brand and your bank account on your own terms.

DON'T WAIT
JOIN TODAY AT:

www.facebook.com/groups/brandhustle

TABLE OF CONTENTS

ACKNOWLEDGMENTS

Every time I have a book published, I sit in awe and wonder. Not only am I a bestselling author, but there are dozens of women, who have trusted me with their stories and their brands, and we have become collective bestsellers. This book is dedicated to all the women, who have allowed me to coach them over the years and were courageous enough to invest in my expertise and their paths to success.

I would like to take some time to acknowledge the small army of people who keep me climbing to the next level. First on the list is Team Jai!

I can't leave out my "same mother" sisters—Jocelyn, Zita, and Rhonda—who are more ride or die than you could ever imagine. I'm throwing in my only brother, Russel, too. (Thanks for those "baby sis" check-ins.)

Also, I acknowledge all my strategic partners who don't mind sharing resources and knowledge.

Finally, my late parents, Russel and Daisy, who gave me the courage to go after my dreams and the confidence to believe that I could achieve them.

FOREWORD

Finding success usually isn't an overnight journey. It takes lots of hard work and failed attempts to find a winning formula that you can bet the farm on. The great thing about discovering the winning formula is that you can duplicate your success and gain exponential results in the process.

Your success can't stop with you. You have a responsibility to create results beyond your own backyard, and you do that by sharing your formula with the masses.

Over the past 16 years, I've had the pleasure of working with some amazing women who have had game-changing accomplishments, and it has been my honor to help them document their success formula. These formulas range from business success, to lifestyle, to financial stability. This book was written specifically to share those roadmaps with readers like you.

I hope we inspire you to document your formula and share your success.

Jai Stone

THE BADASS BIZ TOOLKIT

Jai Stone

It's no secret that I started my branding career working with some of the most recognizable brands in the world. But in the last few years, I have focused on solopreneurs who simply want to create a personal empire that gives them control over their quality of life.

The best way to gain that control is by using technology to scale your business. I'm going to just jump right into this chapter by hitting you right between the eyes. If you are content with the idea that you "don't DO technology," then you can just skip to the next chapter. I can't help you get to the next level. Technology is becoming a bigger part of our daily lives, and it's not going to slow down because you don't want to get onboard. Whew! Now that I got that small rant out of my system, I want to say that women and minorities have a lot of catching up to do to close the digital divide, and now is the time to start.

If you have followed me online, you probably have heard my story of going broke and rebuilding my business to six figures in 18 months. And no doubt you read about my seven-step strategy that I used to accomplish this task called the Badass Brand Profit System. (Read my chapter in The Formula Volume 1.) Now, let's focus on some of the tools that I used to help me cross the finish line. In this chapter, I will share **13 essential tools** that I use in my day-to-day business.

In order to scale your business, you need to utilize systems (technology) and processes. Let me break down processes first.

PROCESS SYSTEMS

When I say that EVERYTHING needs a documented process, I mean EVERYTHING. Every repetitive project, task, or step in your business needs documented step-by-step instructions. Those steps are what I am referring to when I say processes. This is also called SOPs (Standard Operating Procedures).

Let's give you some other basic definitions to clear up the muck.

PROJECT: A service that happens for a specific period with specific start and ending criteria (dates, deliverables, etc.)

TASK: A directive that is to be accomplished

STEP: The action that needs to be completed to accomplish a task

In my business, I use two platforms to manage my processes:

1. Teamwork (Client Project Management) - $50 Monthly

Teamwork (TW) allows me to communicate with clients and vendors in the same place while tracking the status of a project. It also allows me to hold everyone on the project accountable for communication in regard to tasks. I love the desktop version, but the app sucks major a$$ (lol). Most people use the "TASK" function in TW as well, but my team found it to be cumbersome and time-consuming. Therefore, we use...

2. Meister Task (Internal Task Manager) - Free

This is a task management system on steroids. It allows Team Jai to create tasks then include a checklist of steps that need to be completed to accomplish the tasks. It also allows for comments on the task and allows you to assign the task to someone or watch the task for updates. And I love that it allows us to create a checklist template for repetitive tasks. Both the app and desktop versions are spectacular.

3. Process Street (Process Documentation System) - $15 per month per user

This system allows you to document more complex processes with step-by-step instructions, checklists, videos, and screenshots. You can use LastPass to give your entire team access to a master account.

Now, let's move into the technology stuff.

COMMUNICATION SYSTEMS

Team Jai is a virtual workforce with a few members in other countries. That, coupled with the fact that I travel quite a bit, means that the team and I need to be in contact with each other consistently and at times quickly. For this reason, we use a few different communication tools.

1. Zoom Meeting (Video Conferencing) - Free

Our daily meeting is held via Zoom. This is our version of morning meetings that happen in most companies. We meet at 8:30 a.m. EST, Monday through Thursday. This platform allows us to use laptops or other mobile devices if necessary. It works well because the real-time, on-screen interactions allow my team to see each other and establish a rapport. Zoom also allows us to share our screen in order to share visual tasks. But we can't sit on Zoom all day, so for quick communication, we use...

2. Band (Internal Team Group Chat) - Free

This monster texting platform was initially designed for music groups but has quickly made its way into competitive sports and non-profits. I tested about six different platforms before I fell in love with this one. It allows you to send messages via text, video, audio, or images. It also syncs with Google Calendar. This keeps us from having to share personal cell numbers. I love that this has both an app and a desktop version.

3. Grasshopper (Phone System) - $26 Monthly

This is a cost-effective telephone service that I have used off and on for about ten years. It allows my team to call or text clients without using their personal phone service. I also love the app for on-the-go use, and the desktop platform is easy to use for more complex updates to your company registry.

4. Facebook Messenger (Event Group Chat) - Free

When I host events, it's important for all the stilettos on the ground to keep up with each other. Since most people have a Facebook account, it is easy to just add them to a group chat without too much fuss or intrusion. When the event is over, simply delete the chat.

COMMUNITY BUILDING TOOLS

A big part of why my marketing strategies are so successful is because of my relationship with my community. You can't just up and ask folks to buy your sh*t and you haven't spoken to them in six months. Here are the platforms I use to keep in touch with my audience:

5. Active Campaign (External Email to Clients) - $15 Monthly

This is a power-packed marketing platform that I use to do everything from delivering my free eBooks to sending out weekly notes. With the click of a few buttons, I can send an email to thousands of people. What I love most is that I was able to train Team Jai to use it in two short sessions. And YES... it is more powerful than MailChimp and easier to use than Infusionsoft.

6. Facebook Groups - Free

We use FB groups for several of our projects and online communities. Again, most people have a Facebook account and are familiar with posting, commenting, etc. This allows us a more interactive way to communicate with our online audience and customers.

PRODUCTION SYSTEMS

One of the major reasons that businesses will find success is based on how productive the staff is. In order to keep my team productive, I use the following tools:

1. G Suite by Google (Email & Calendar) - $5 Monthly (per account)

This solution allows me to use my own domain on the Gmail platform. It gives my domain seamless integration with other Google properties like You-Tube. And the calendar is universal to sync. What I love most is the Master Admin account that gives me control over all email addresses in my domain. I do NOT use Google Drive for storage because it requires that my external clients have a Gmail account to gain access. Instead we use...

2. Box.com (Online File Storage) - $5 Monthly

I love many things about this online file storage system, starting with the fact that it uploads and downloads at twice the speed of Dropbox and Google Drive. I also love the fact that my clients don't need an account to access files; they simply need the hyperlink. While the solution can get pricey once you increase the external access levels, it's been well worth the cost for me. Did I mention that the app is awesome too?

3. Microsoft Office Suite (Word, PowerPoint, Excel) - $99 annually per user

The Office Suite is an old standard for me because it is universal. Sure, there are other production suites out there that work similarly, but you will always run into a compatibility issue when opening or editing documents. That kind of thing can put a major kink in your productions.

4. LASTPASS Teams (Password Manager) - $4 monthly per user

If you are anything like me, you have a bazillion passwords. It's next to impossible to keep up with them, so you need a password manager. But Last-Pass does more than that. It allows you to share your login access with your team without giving out your sensitive password data. This has saved me from security breaches and endless hours of changing passwords.

That's my top 13 list of tools you need. I know when you start to look at the costs I've listed, things add up. But think about it this way: you can't build a million-dollar brand off of a two-dollar mindset.

Booyah!

To learn about other tools and systems I use to grow my brand, become a part of my Brand & Hustle online community visit: Facebook.com/BrandHustle

THE SAVVY HIRING FORMULA

Sabrina Alridge-Moore: SAM

Life often throws you a curve ball. The question I have for you is: what is your next move? Do you return the serve or just let it fall off to the wayside? This is what I call a forced or an inevitable foul. I have gone back and forth as to where my story starts. What point in my journey do I think is meaningful enough to share?

I've always had this soft inner voice and desire to do my own thing, but for one reason or another, be it my family, fear, doubt, or uncertainty, I have moved away from doing my own thing. I've honestly been afraid of the unknown. However, if I had to pick a definitive point when my eyes were truly opened, then I would tell you three years ago.

In 2015, I was laid off from a major oil and gas company. Now, I won't lie. It was a gut-wrenching experience. I had never been laid off before. Plus, I had finally found what I thought was the company that I would retire from. Without a doubt, this organization not only had the culture and values that I desired my entire career, but I was working with a team of individuals that I really liked. My whole world shattered, leaving me with so many emotions—anger, embarrassment, and self-doubt, just to name a few.

I say all of that to bring us here. You know the old saying, "Everything happens for a reason?" It's true! I met one of the most amazing women who I now affectionately refer to as my business bestie and my sister from another mother. She was at a crossroad with her job as well. That's when me and my business bestie partnered up and became each other's rock and confidant. We started our first business venture together called "Wife Life Today." During this time, we met Jai Stone. Jai recommended that we separate and do our own individual businesses which resulted in the birth of my business, SAM the HRSavvyPro!

I am a firm believer that every person on this earth has the right to provide for not only themselves but also for their families. So, I am now taking my more than twenty years of talent acquisition and human resources experience to train and consult with organizations, enabling them to foster a more diverse workforce and reduce turnover. I have some primary principles that will help a company start to pave the way to not only hire diverse employees but to retain them as well. So, if you are ready, let's get to work with five primary pointers that I call Five to Thrive!

THE SAVVY HIRING FORMULA

1. Create an environment in the workplace where innovation is valued and incorporated.

When a person's ideas are not just heard but really received, that can go a very long way when it comes to fostering and diversifying relationships within the organization. Hold brainstorming sessions and town hall meetings. Start by having meetings, then follow through by implementing some of their ideas. Recognize employees for contributing. This not only gets their buy-in but will also help to create more lengthy tenure.

2. Apply the golden rule.

It is basic human behavior 101; our core desire is to be treated with respect. If we are being honest, most people do not walk around being mean and disrespectful to others intentionally. However, more likely than not, people live by the rule of "you have to give respect to get it." The reviews that an organization receives on reporting sites does, can, and will impact their brand.

3. Implement multi-cultural events.

Encourage employees to share some of their cultural practices. Get involved and sponsor cultural events—not only within the organization but also in the communities that you operate within. It's simple really. When employees see you investing in their communities, showing a true respect and willingness to learn about their world, it's amazing what happens. There is an unspoken loyalty that is created, which makes it tougher for employees to be easily wooed away.

4. Be aware of employee stressors

More often than not, we compare ourselves to others. Most people will not admit this openly, but whether you will admit it or not, taking on projects and meeting or surpassing KPIs (Key Performance Indicators) is stressful. Employees who have a diverse culture or background sometime feel an obligation to take on more work, so they can (at the bare minimum) run the race with their counterparts. Often, it is more than they should ever take on which can result in an emotional and physical downhill spiral. If this happens, there will inevitably be a decrease in productivity which means a decrease in revenue flow.

5. Do what you say you are going to do!

Don't just talk about it be about it. Employees not only want to see what the organization plans to do but how and when they are going to go about it. Yes, employees what to see that change management is implemented, but more importantly, they want to see that it is continued and becomes part of the organization's core.

BONUS:
IMPLEMENT A WORK MENTOR PROGRAM

The goal is for it not be a one-sided relationship. Everyone has a responsibility to be a mentor to the other; they will learn by way of sharing differences, ideas, and getting to know each other on a personal level.

- When employees get to know each other on a personal level, no matter their background and culture, it will help them discover commonalties which will expand their appreciation for their differences. The results will stimulate a more inclusive and friendly work environment.

SAM'S FIVE STEP COMPANY CHECK:

1. Run your compliance numbers.

- Identify where the company is coming up short and devise a plan to rectify it.

2. Map out what your ideal organization looks like.

- Where would you like to see the company in two years?

3. **Poll your employees for what they do and don't like and what they want.**

   - After all feedback submitted, we will categorize what employees want and give it to them!

4. **Create a ZERO tolerance for retaliation.**

   - We are going to charge leaders with fostering an environment where their direct reports feel comfortable with asking questions and not have their inquisitiveness viewed as challenging their authority.

5. **Hire SAM the HRSavvyPro (by visiting www. hrsavvyro.com/services)**

   - SAM will work with you to create strategies that can be implemented to be expeditiously impactful.

   - SAM will map out what your organization's future diversity blueprint looks like.

   - Don't be afraid of what they have to say.

     i. SAM's help and the feedback received are going to be used to your company's advantage.

- With SAM's guidance, the fear of retaliation will be removed from the work environment.

Contending with how to build up their employees' talents and expand the diversity of their staff is something that most leaders are tasked with on a regular basis. The million-dollar question is where do we go to find and hire the most diverse candidates?

QUICK POINTERS:

- Keep an eye out for good talent (that star employee).
- Be unorthodox in your approach; go against the grain.
  - Sometimes you must make people uncomfortable to arrive at a comfortable solution.
- Get in the trenches with your employees.
- Strive for a minimum of two hires in every area of diversity.
- Educate people on "unconscious bias." Partner with the training department because studies show that people hire like people.
- Meet with leaders and talent acquisition employees to discuss diversity goals and strategies.

- Encourage employees to have conversations about diversity within reason, even though it is a delicate subject. Walking around it on eggshells as if it does not exist only creates more tension. However, if conversations do take place, it can play a significant part in eradicating biases and breaking down barriers that keep diversity and inclusion from flourishing in the workplace.

- Partner with other diversity organizations to become a sponsor for events at a local, state, and even national level.

NEXT STEP: PLAN FOR THE EMPLOYER

Project

Lead

Agile

New

As an employer, SAM will charge you to:

Project and create a plan.

Lead the organization through the changes.

To be **Agile** and nimble throughout the process,

And to have a **New** mindset and approach.

Disclaimer: None of this will be easy, but please remember that you are never going to please all your employees all the time. As long as you can please some of them most of the time, you are on the right track.

Challenge: Stop blending in and do your part to challenge and change the status quo. Will your company be the organization that transitions the view and standards of the employee-to-employer relationship? Will your company take a stance and put their mark on the world?

Question: Is your organization finally sick and tired of being sick and tired?

Let's get to work!

THE PROPEL YOUR PROFITS FORMULA

Sha' Cannon

Get profits from your purpose. That buzz phrase has many disillusioned entrepreneurs thinking all they have to do is figure out their purpose and soon thereafter the profits will come rolling in. There are even business coaches who offer programs to take you from "purpose to profits." It all sounds so awesome. You know what's not awesome? The reality that you can be great at what you do and your business still not bring in the money you need to sustain that business—let alone make a profit.

Creating revenue in your business (making money from the offerings of your business) is very different than making enough money to cover your business expenses and fund your lifestyle. You see, a profit is an overage of money left after you have paid all your expenses. Commonly, entrepreneurs are not creating enough money in their business to see a profit. Sadly, most of those entrepreneurs give up on their dream of entrepreneurship before they can successfully make a profit within their business.

I left corporate America and a total income of six figures on October 20, 2017 to become a full-time entrepreneur. I had been working my business on a part-time basis for four years before going full-time. I had clients who paid me for services, but I was not making a profit. I invested more into my business than I received out of my business. In fact, my corporate job fully funded my entrepreneurial efforts. From marketing to technology to business events to coaching... you name it, I invested in my business from the income obtained by working my job.

At the point that I decided to leave a stable six-figure income behind for the uncertainty of entrepreneurship, I had just received a contract with a retainer client to add to the revenue from sporadic publishing clients. With a contract covering two-thirds of the income I'd lose, I figured it was now or never to really turn my focus to my business full-time.

I took that leap of faith, and it took faith to keep me going. At that point in my life, I was no longer used to budgeting, making financial sacrifices, worrying about bills, etc. BUT those were the very things that became my new reality. My entrepreneurial path revealed itself as I walked it. However, it unfolded extremely close to my feet at times and that caused a lot of stress for me.

Whether you have business besties or you attend events with other entrepreneurs, you've heard stories like mine before. Enough about the problem! What's the solution? Propel your profits by creating diverse streams of income in your business. Let's talk about what that looks like.

Here are my four strategies for creating diverse streams of income:

- Create a pipeline to filter clients to your main products and services.
- Create a way to open your business model.
- Create strategic partnerships.
- Create different paths to the same results.

THE PROPEL YOUR PROFITS FORMULA

FORMULA

Strategy #1: Create a pipeline to filter clients to your main products and services. Offering publication services such as editing and formatting to independent authors were the main offerings of my business. It became increasingly hard to find independent authors to target for my services. Fewer prospects to tell about my services meant I sold my services to fewer and fewer people. I came to realize that not many people believed they could write a book. I ran into potential clients every day who needed to write a book to boost their credibility. They agreed that being a published author was a great tool to cement their expertise. However, they believed that writing a book was an unattainable goal for them. See a gap, fill the gap, right? I set on a path to create a program that would teach first-time authors how to write their books and support them on their writing journey. I created a four-week group program and named it Bookocity. The result of this program was a full book draft for first-time authors who did the work. All successful clients of this program were then filtered into my publication services. Viola, more profit! I created a pipeline that resulted in clients for my main service.

How can you create potential clients for your main product or service with another "prequel" service that positions them to be ideal to purchase your main product or service as a next step?

Strategy #2: Create a way to open your business model. I created content for my business that provided education on the publication industry which demystified a lot of the unknown about writing and self-publishing books. That content increased my visibility and put me on the radar of a lot of potential clients. It also had fellow entrepreneurs not interested in writing a book to want to know how I always created content that spoke to my ideal avatar and prompted them to engage with me on that content and publicly declare they would like to work with me. Due to this demand, I realized that I could open my business model to include content creation in my business offerings. You see, a book is simply a large piece of content. Blog posts, social media posts, and live streaming are smaller pieces of content. I was able to tie the two together by showing clients how to use a book to pull out content for blog posts, social media posts, etc. Bam, more profit! I opened my business model to include related offerings that made sense to my ideal client avatars.

What service or product can you include in your business model that the clients you already attract can use but still makes sense for what you already offer?

Strategy #3: Create strategic partnerships. A great deal of entrepreneurs market to and service individuals. What I mean by that is they offer their product or service to be purchased by one person at a time. Even when I created group programs, I still marketed to individuals to fill the groups. I had to get smart. What's better than selling to individuals? Selling to groups, of course. I partnered with business coaches who taught strategy to help their clients create eBooks to position their expertise and develop a low price point product to allow potential clients to get familiar with the value that they as the expert offered. The coaches' clients were able to leave their programs with something tangible, an eBook, to accompany the intangible skills and strategies that they learned from the coaching program. Boom, more profit! I took a service that I offered to individuals and partnered with another business to offer the same service to a group of their clients.

How can you take a service or product and offer it in bulk to another business for use with their clients?

Strategy #4: Create different paths to the same results. Some entrepreneurs start off with a signature service—one offering. It's great to be known for one thing before you branch off into different things. As you have read, I was known for publication services before I started to offer content creation services. However, when I only offered publication services, I offered these services in different ways:

- I taught a live workshop to teach clients how to write a book and how to navigate the world of self-publication.

- I wrote a book on how to write a book and one on how to self-publish a book.

- I created the group coaching program, Bookocity, to help first-time authors write their book draft.

- I created an eCourse called *Make Me an Amazon Best-selling Author* to educate first-time authors on the strategies used to become Amazon bestselling authors.

That is just four examples of offerings in different formats that my ideal clients can purchase from me, all under the same umbrella of publication. Pow, more profit! I created products that complimented the services that I offered to appeal to my same target audience in different ways. In return, I created more opportunities for more people to purchase from me.

How can you take a singular offering and re-create it in different formats for purchase by a wider variety of your ideal clients?

Thanks to these strategies my business is more financially stable and turning a profit. At the end of the day, the more opportunities we create for clients to spend money with us the more money we make and the more our profits increase!

THE 30-DAY ACTION PLAN FORMULA

Yolanda V. Cornelius

Bold, highly driven, assertive, focused—words used repeatedly to describe me at one point or another throughout my twenties. I never set out to build that persona, but after eight years of service in the United States Army, it was who I had become. Mind, body and soul. I embraced it wholeheartedly. I took pride in my image and worked my ass off to live up to the expectations that came along with it. By the time I was in my thirties, my confidence was through the roof. No longer was I the skinny, confused teenage mom trying to finish high school, but I was now a strong, black woman with an accounting degree who loved the skin I was in.

My career was thriving just like I planned, and I was headed for a long-term relationship with success. At least, I appeared to be until I encountered a series of life-altering events. It started with my mom being diagnosed with stage IV colon cancer when I was thirty-two, my daughter's announcement that she was expecting a baby when I was thirty-three, then the request for my resignation from my position the week after I returned from my mother's funeral. By then, I was thirty-four. Talk about a series of WTF moments...*way too far.* I truly had no idea what to do next.

Over the next few years, I watched my personal, professional, and financial lives take a complete 180-degree turn. Between the ages of thirty-five and thirty-nine, I was laid off two more times, depleted the last of the funds in my 401k, filed bankruptcy twice (once to save my home from foreclosure), became a grandmother of four, supported my father through his massive heart attack, and accepted a 14,000 dollar pay cut to get a permanent full-time position after the layoffs.

My forties started out the same way my thirties ended. By this point, I was mentally and emotionally exhausted, not to mention tired of being broke. I found myself living on the cusp of fuckery. You know that point when any and everything that goes wrong makes you wonder if you're being punished for something you did long ago.

At any rate, I took a second job for the umpteenth time thinking it was my next best move. While working my part-time job, I met a woman who was also working the two-job hustle like me. After a few conversations and lifestyle comparisons, we seemed to have a lot in common. She revealed that she had worked two jobs for the past twenty years. I remember thinking, "Twenty years with two jobs?" Who does that? Why not hone your skills and find *one* better paying job instead of working two? However, she was content and proud of her two-job status. I, on the other hand, was not. I was tired of going down this path every time I encountered a professional or financial crisis. I quickly realized with each conversation between us that if I didn't shift soon, her story would become my story, and I would also have twenty years in the two-job hustle game.

From that moment forward, I *committed* to no more part-time jobs. It was time to SHIFT, and I was ready! Over the next year, I did just that. I focused on advancing my career, shifted my mindset from acknowledging change to adapting to change, and changed my life thirty days at a time. I set and achieved SMART goals every thirty days until I was literally able to think, shift, plan, and execute my way to getting a new position, doubling my income, and publishing my first self-help book, *Fit, Fabulous and Focused: How to Create the Life You Want After Forty*.

THE 30-DAY ACTION PLAN FORMULA

Building a thirty-day action plan was more than just gathering my thoughts and ideas and writing them in my journal. It required planning and strategy. My strategy involves four components: Think, Shift, Plan and Execute. This is known as my 30-day Smart Action Formula. I've included a few guidelines below to start you on your way to building your very own 30-day smart action formula.

WEEK 1: THINK (GET SPECIFIC)

The process involves strategic thinking. This type of thinking is succinct, deliberate, and should yield a specific result. The key to strategic thinking is to create an environment or space that allows you to think without interruption.

- **Declutter your zone.** Prepare your space for thinking. Add candles, pens, notepads, and highlighters. Create a space that visually helps others respect your time and honor your designated space.

- **Block distractions.** Disconnect from your day. Turn off the TV, social media, cable, and satellite television. Silence your phones and texts during this time. Avoid multi-tasking and distractions while you are thinking strategically.

- **Make it a priority.** Set aside time to think. Add a daily appointment on your calendar and make this time a priority. Keep your appointment time for the same time and the same space.

- **Identify your "one thing."** What will make the most impact in your personal, professional, or financial life within the next thirty days? Keep in mind, thirty days is not a long period of time, so the more specific you can be the better it will be for you.

- **Write down your desired outcome.** Once you identify your "one thing" that you will achieve, write it down. Make it plain and look at it daily.

WEEK 2: SHIFT (BUILD MOMENTUM)

Building a thirty-day action plan requires you to build and maintain momentum. This typically requires a change in your daily habits and public commitment to your routine.

- **Honor your workspace.** Once you have claimed your workspace, make it yours. Show up at the same space...every day... every time when it's time to work. It shows your level of commitment and garners a respect for your personal time.

- **Publicly commit to your decision.** Get buy-in and support from your family, friends, and team. Make them a part of your journey. This might improve accountability as you develop your action plan.

- **Delegate duties and eliminate excuses.** The more often you delegate daily tasks such as household chores and errands the less excuses you will make as you shift your priorities. Delegate tasks and set clear expectations. Have frequent and candid conversations to ensure things are happening the way you need them to happen as you pursue your goal.

- **Say no and set boundaries.** Set expectations and stick to them. Know your priorities. Get comfortable with communicating your intentions to others and staying focused on your goals.

WEEK 3: PLAN (CREATE ACCOUNTABILITY)

When building an action plan, the tiniest details can cause significant problems if they are overlooked. This process may require some research to ensure that you are not omitting tasks from your new endeavor.

- **List action steps.** List the exact steps it will take to achieve your goal. Every task, no matter how small or insignificant, should be included. Create a schedule of all the action steps required to achieve your goal. After you've built your action plan, repeat this process to ensure that you have not omitted any steps.

- **Identify the uncontrollable.** In every plan, there are uncontrollable factors that you might encounter. The key to a successful action plan is knowing what those potential factors are in advance so that you can adjust as needed. List the uncontrollable and discuss them with your team often.

- **Identify the resources needed**. Who and how will you achieve your goal? How much money will you need? Do you have to rent additional space? Need a larger vehicle? Do you have the required expertise and certifications required to achieve your goal? What additional systems and processes do you need to implement? Have you identified the members of your team?

- **Establish accountability.** Accountability is achieved *after* you have identified the action steps and the resources needed. Assign each task in the action plan to a specific team member. Put the assigned tasks in writing and communicate it to your entire team. This process will set expectations, reduce confusion, and create accountability.

- **Set milestones.** What are the significant highpoints and checkpoints of your plan? Recognizing these moments as they happen throughout your plan will help measure the success and completion of your action plan.

WEEK 4: EXECUTE (MAKE SHIFT HAPPEN)

"Every minute you spend in planning saves you ten minutes in execution; this gives you a 1000 percent return on energy."
–Brian Tracy

If you spent your first three weeks building a solid plan, then week four should be solely dedicated to execution.

- **Focus on results not activity.** Focus on doing fewer things very well. Avoid getting distracted by activities that divert you from your action plan. Stick to your action plan by focusing on measurable milestones and results.

- **Utilize systems and processes.** It can be very beneficial if you allow the systems and processes you put in place to work for you. Some of those benefits include time savings, increased productivity, and increased revenues.

- **Solicit and give feedback.** Communication is key. As you execute your action plan, ensure that you are open to feedback from your team. This will create a culture of honest and open communication. It will also minimize mistakes during execution.

- **Partner and collaborate.** Depending on the extent of your action plan, you may have to collaborate or partner with others to get things done. Ensure that you have buy-in from all parties involved before executing your plan. Communicate your expectations clearly and get all agreements in writing.

- **Repurpose your team as needed.** There may be times that you find a team member's abilities are not effectively aligned with the tasks you've assigned in your action plan. Do not hesitate to address this immediately. A simple tweak or adjustment can be the difference between the success and the failure of your action plan.

When it's all said and done, a properly executed action plan can propel you forward personally, financially, or professionally.

To find out more about my thirty-day action plan strategy and how I can help you, visit my website at www.yolandav.com

BUILDING BRAND AUTHORITY THROUGH PODCASTING FORMULA

Dr. Nii-Daako Darko

Let me get real with you. As a kid, I always wanted to have an impact on people or be larger than life. I thought about becoming an astronaut, athlete, lawyer, or doctor. It wasn't until I was introduced to Dr. Heathcliff Huxtable on television that I knew what I wanted to be, a successful doctor with a beautiful wife, great kids, and live in Brooklyn. What more could a regular kid from New York City want?

Over time, I got the degrees, credentials, and certifications. Mission accomplished! I finally became what I had been chasing for half my life, a trauma surgeon. Quickly, I realized that my life was far from a TV show. I had done countless surgeries and saved hundreds of lives, but I couldn't do something as simple as take an extended vacation with my family or make it to my nephew's high school football game. As a doctor, not only was I not in complete control over my life, but I also hadn't explored other talents I knew I had. I was in a box.

After a year of doing locum tenens work, I had met so many doctors making moves outside of traditional medicine. There were doctors who did medical humanitarian work in war-torn places of the world, others running their own businesses, and some were on television.

They were happy and passionate not just about being physicians but about being IMPACTFUL and adding VALUE to society by doing more than just medicine.

I thought to myself, "If I had known some of these stories or met these people during my climb up the ladder, maybe I would have done things a bit differently." At the same time, with over $662,000 in student loan debt, I was consuming podcasts to learn more about debt and personal finance. I was shocked that I couldn't find podcasts centered around doctors who were thriving in non-traditional careers. So, I pulled my other talents off the back burner and created *Docs Outside the Box* podcast.

Docs Outside the Box podcast brings stories of ordinary doctors doing extraordinary things to inspire other docs to think outside the box. My guests are living proof that doctors can break free from the exam room. Since starting the podcast two years ago, the show has been consistently in the Top 100 in the careers section of Apple Podcasts. I have been asked to speak at conferences and featured in numerous "Best of" lists. Without a doubt, podcasting has been the number one way that I have been able to develop brand authority as "The Doc Outside the Box."

Ever wondered what more you could be, what more you can do? Put on your headphones, jump in front of a mic and join me on the podcast movement.

3, 2, 1 . . . PODCAST - A BEGINNER'S GUIDE TO BUILDING BRAND AUTHORITY THROUGH PODCASTING

In case you have been living under a rock for the past couple of years, podcasting has been the fastest growing digital media form. Podcasting originated around the early 2000s when iPods were the craze and people downloaded digital audio files to them and other mobile devices. They are like internet radio shows on demand. Technology has made it both easy and cheap to start a podcast. As a result, everybody and their mother are making a podcast, and the trend doesn't seem to be fading anytime soon.

Check out these statistics[1]:

- In 2016, over 100 million people have listened to a podcast.

1 http://www.convinceandconvert.com/podcast-research/the-11-critical-podcast-statistics-of-2017/

- Over 50 million Americans listen to podcasts monthly.

- 42 million Americans listen to podcasts weekly (that is five times more than who go to the movies!).

THE PODCASTING FORMULA

WHAT'S YOUR TOPIC?

A governing body for podcasts doesn't exist. That means that nobody determines if there are too many podcasts on how hip-hop culture for cats exists. Just a joke, but catch my drift? What you talk about and where you go with your show is almost limitless within the world of podcasting.

Once you have a topic in mind, you will need an actual name for your podcast. Be unique with the name you choose because the last thing you want is another podcaster accusing you of copyright or trademark infringement. Also, the shorter the name, the better. Like most memorable television shows or movies, keep the name to three or four words maximum. Once again, roam the podcast directories to ensure that your name is not taken.

TOOLS

- **Microphone:** A good microphone can make or break the audio listening process. Stay away from using the standard microphone with your laptop or desktop. A fan favorite among podcasters is the Audio-Technica ATR2100 USB. It's portable, it doesn't pick up a lot of ambient noise, and it's not too expensive.

- **Headphones:** A good set of headphones will go a long way for both recording and editing your podcast. Headphones are very useful because they prevent feedback between your speakers and microphone which can cause a poor listening experience for your audience.

- **Laptop or Desktop Computer:** Gone are the days of needing a studio and a producer to create an audio experience that listeners will like. As long as you have a laptop, desktop, or even a cell phone-- you're golden.

- **Editing Software:** Editing a podcast is not rocket science. As a matter of fact, depending on what kind of computer you are using (Mac vs. PC), there are free software options available to you. For Mac users, Garage Band already comes pre-installed and is simple enough for most beginners. On the PC side, Audacity is a free downloadable software that has become the go-to for many podcasters, including me.

HOSTING

Think of hosting as a place where listeners can easily access your content 24/7/365. There is a difference between your website and podcast hosting. Believe it or not, your website cannot handle the traffic of continuous downloading of mp3 files. That experience would create a very slow-loading website not only for you but also for other customers who have websites on the same servers as you. Not only that, but you could incur a lot of fees for allowing users to download files from your website. To get around this, podcast hosting sites were created to store the audio files, while your website points users to the podcast hosting site for the actual downloading of the file.

FORMATTING

- **Length:** Is there a sweet spot for the length of the show? Nobody truly knows, but in today's world of shorter attention spans, shorter is always better! In my opinion, keeping the show to less than an hour is great. And if you keep the show to thirty minutes or less, you're golden!

- **Intro:** This is your chance to stand out. Claim your space in the podcasting world and be unique with your introduction. Whether it's a catchy phrase, jingle, or rap--this is your chance to energize your audience and let them know what your show is all about. If you decide to use music in your intro, please make sure that the music is royalty free.

- **Main Segment:** This is the meat and potatoes of the show. My advice is to think of your show like a television show that has different segments.

- **Outro:** Whew, you made it to the end of your show! Capitalize on this opportunity by creating a call to action. A call to action is something you want your listeners to do at the end of the show (e.g. subscribing to your show, sharing episodes with others, and sending in questions). A call to action is a powerful tool to help your show grow.

INTERVIEW

Performing an interview on a podcast is not like interviewing someone for a job. People often ask me, "What's the best way to conduct an interview?" My answer is always, "Just think of all the things you want to learn from this person, but picture yourself having a pizza or coffee with them." I prefer to keep things chill. More than likely, your guests have never been on a podcast before, and they'll look to you for guidance. So, if you're nervous, guess what? They're going to be nervous and stiff, and ultimately the interview will come off to the audience as dull.

GUESTS

Guests can make or break your show. Always think about what will bring value to your listeners. If your show is about hip-hop for cats, inviting Tony Robbins to be a guest probably won't go over well. If your show is about personal finance and investing, then getting Tony Robbins would be a huge score. Not all guests are the same. Some do well with written work or well-choreographed productions. As a result, they may come off as boring on a podcast.

SCHEDULE

One thing that I will stress in this book more than anything else is to be consistent. Whether you have five listeners or two hundred thousand, your listeners want to be confident that your show will consistently show up in their inboxes. Don't worry too much about downloads and statistics yet. Be more concerned with having a reliable schedule because that helps to build anticipation for your show and ultimately leads to growth in listenership.

You made it! This is a bit to digest, but you've just taken a huge jump towards developing the platform and brand authority you have always been looking for. Don't let this be where your momentum stops; I'm here for you. Connect with me at www. drniidarko.com. If all you need is just inspiration, then check out my parting words for my audience on my podcast: **"We only got one life. Let's make it count and live outside the box!"**

THE CUSTOMER CONNECTION FORMULA

Chris Davis

Growing your business boils down to your ability to do one thing: continually get people to show up with interest and act on their interest. From paid advertising to organic growth, the goal has always been to identify interested people and introduce them to your business. But honestly, that's just the start. Once they show up, how do you turn those new people into customers? Once they're customers, how do you keep them coming back? If you really want to grow, how do you enable those new customers to recruit more customers? The key to your business growth is hidden within the answers to those questions.

Business growth is a phrase, a term that is often thrown out there quickly and easily, but the business owners know little about exactly what it takes to build and grow a business. And there's a lot. It's a big process in getting your business up and running. And businesses, if you look at it, especially if you're bootstrapping, can only be built one brick at a time. Some days you'll lay ten bricks; some days you'll struggle just locating the pile of bricks. This is the journey for the entrepreneur. To navigate through the tough terrain of business establishment and growth and come out on the other side having found success is what businesses want to do. The goal is a continual forward progression towards business growth which is why it is extremely important to ensure that the proper expectations are set before you start the journey. In fact, your biggest frustrations in business, and in life, will come from when your reality doesn't match your expectations.

So, as you continue to read this chapter, it's important to be able to identify exactly what it takes to generate the revenue that you desire, and to build your business in a way that can continually achieve it. I want you to be able to have the confidence in your business that you know it's working, and you can hit a button and make it work again.

I'm oversimplifying, but you get the point. As you continue, know that the words written come from being on the "marketing battlefield." This is not from the sidelines taking notes; it's from playing in the game. Sometimes on the winning team, a lot of times on the losing. But always learning, adjusting, and optimizing along the way. As I currently operate as the Director of Education at a tech startup called Active Campaign, a small business marketing automation tool platform, I also have had the opportunity to train and teach hundreds of businesses this same effective approach to marketing. I know when it comes to why I'm in this space it was not by happenstance. This is very much intentional. Not only do I love automation, I love seeing businesses grow through the effective use of technology. I hope that in reading this chapter, you see the value in it as well.

THE CUSTOMER CONNECTION FORMULA

THE SYSTEMS

There are five systems present in every business that are responsible for producing results. A system is defined as a set of processes organized for a desired outcome. Processes, simply put, are how you get things done. If processes are the way that you get things done in your business and those processes create systems, you can now see the role systems play in your business.

Systems are responsible for executing your business marketing strategy. Or in other words, systems are responsible for getting things done. All growth in digital marketing relies on your ability to properly implement technology to create automated systems that continually execute your marketing strategy for you.

That may take a bit to sink in, so just remember that getting things done with technology is what you're aiming to figure out. Technology won't be able to do everything for you nor should you rely on it to. But brought in for the right processes, it will yield great results.

It is important for you to not only understand these systems (so you know what to build), but also how they function, especially since they are present in every business. In the next sections, I'll identify each system for your permanent understanding.

System 1 - Traffic System

Traffic is your ability to raise awareness and interest in your product. This is often referred to as "traffic generation." It's turning someone who has no clue about your business into someone who is interested and will potentially pay you for your product.

The most common practice is to create blog posts around topics that are of interest to the people you would like to convert into customers. Their presence on your website (reading an article, for instance) is what is referred to as traffic. Think of traffic as the blood running through your business. No blood, no business.

System 2 - Capture System

The second system is your capture system which is responsible for capitalizing on the traffic you have generated. This often takes place on a landing page where you provide something free in value (referred to as a Lead magnet or Irresistible Free Offer) in exchange for the visitor's information. The key here is to reduce as much friction as possible in the decision-making process. Your offer should speak so clearly that it becomes a no brainer to act by entering their information to get access to it.

The information you capture at this stage will set the tone for how personal you will be able to be in your messaging for the next stage. These two systems are what create your Lead Generation System. It speaks to your ability to raise and capture interest effectively.

I highly recommend, if you were confused by where to get started with digital marketing, to start with these first two systems. They are what will keep new leads flowing through once you get busy with new customers.

System 3 - Follow-Up System

Most businesses are struggling with defining a consistent way of following up with every lead that encounters their business. You cannot afford for this to be true for you and your online efforts, mainly because one of the biggest benefits of using technology in your marketing is that you can continually execute what you need to.

What you need to execute here is following up with every person whose information you capture. This could look different depending on your business model. Some businesses follow up with a phone call while others use email. Some businesses will use a mixed approach of both email and phone call! Whatever the case may be for you, what you want to keep in mind is that this system needs to build trust and educate your leads, so they can easily make an informed buying decision later.

System 4 - Sales System

Your sales system is arguably your most important system. Just as I mentioned the previous systems would be a good starting place for automation, the same cannot be said for your sales system. Since it's responsible for processing payments, you don't want that ability to fail in any capacity. This is your most sensitive system. One wrong tweak here can result in fortunes lost. In contrast, one right tweak here can result in fortunes in the bank.

I would classify all the previous systems as part of your marketing efforts. This system exemplifies the hand off between marketing and sales. As marketing acquires, educates, and qualifies new leads, it hands it off to the sales system to close them. You will want to use technology that makes this handoff as strong as possible.

System 5 - Delivery

Your delivery system is all about immediacy. Any delay between this and your sales system can result in refunds. This speaks to the expectation the digital era has created. People want the information and/or products immediately. Cause someone to wait, and you will cause them to leave your business.

Again, we see this more apparent online than offline when relationship building is not done face-to-face. Thankfully, technology allows us to not only meet this need but also to exceed it. Now you can provide immediate SMS messages on products physically shipped or send login credentials via email within five minutes of purchase. Delivery done right can create immediate evangelists for your brand. It can also create immediate affiliates because it creates immediate satisfaction.

In all these systems in your business, it's your job to understand the processes for each one because they are the employees. They are the ones that make these systems run efficiently. Each system is intertwined with the next, automatically handing off your leads from one to the next. As these leads go through the system, you're collecting more and more information so that when they arrive at the next system, it has been informed with an accurate account of their behavior. This way, you can make their journey as personalized as possible. Remember, personalized marketing produces profits.

CONCLUSION

You are now one step closer, my friends, to automating your marketing and working on your business instead of in it. Take everything that you've read in this book, highlight it, scribble around it, and make notes. Keep this as a resource and a reminder of how you can leverage technology in today's age, which will provide you freedom and flexibility to operate in your business the way you desire—without your revenue suffering.

THE PRICELESS SMILE FORMULA

Dr. Kimberly Harper

The confidence to sell yourself starts with a great smile!

As entrepreneurs, we sell our products and services to others daily. Our marketing plan may include list building, word of mouth, and social media. All of these are great avenues for marketing, but ultimately, what we are selling is ourselves. Whether you think looks should matter or not, they do. Unfortunately, in the business world, how you look says everything about whether you are competent or qualified to do the job. A critical component of an attractive appearance is your smile. Numerous studies have shown that people with straight white teeth are more successful, more capable, more employable, more attractive, wealthier and more educated. This may sound vain, but a beautiful white smile could make a difference in the success of your business.

THE PRICELESS SMILE
FORMULA

I am Dr. Kimberly Harper, a cosmetic and restorative dentist, speaker, and author. I help my patients restore their smiles and regain their confidence, so they can live, love, and laugh without embarrassment. What does confidence mean to you? I believe confidence is our ability to believe in ourselves. As an entrepreneur, what we choose to believe will determine our success and ultimately how much money we can make. There was a time in my life that I didn't believe in myself. I lacked the confidence to do the things I wanted to do.

My weight has been an issue most of my life. Growing up, I was the chubby kid who was ridiculed in school and always picked last in gym class. In my teen years, there were only a few dates and social activities with friends. I chose not to participate in sports or other activities because I felt ashamed and embarrassed of my body. I always felt insecure and lacked the confidence to just be me.

After years of staying home on Friday nights, I decided that enough was enough. It was the summer before my senior year, and I was determined to go to the prom with a date and not a group of friends. So, I started working out daily and tracking my food. Within four months, I lost twenty-five pounds. The feeling was amazing. For the first time in my life, I felt good about myself. I liked what I saw in the mirror, I liked how my clothes fit my body, and I felt comfortable and confident. I went to my senior prom that year with a date. Managing my weight can still be a challenge at times, but one thing I did not lose was my confidence in myself.

Where do you lack confidence? Is it your weight? Your body? Or your smile? If it's your smile, I'm here to help. I created the Priceless Smile Formula to help my patients tackle their dental problems and smile again. This formula helps you regain your confidence in your smile, become the shining success you were created to be, and make more money!

How do you achieve a great smile? There are four steps to achieving a priceless smile:

1. Good oral hygiene
2. Good alignment
3. Good dentist
4. Good treatment plan

Following these four steps will give you the smile of your dreams and the confidence to take on the world. I have completed this formula with several of my dental patients, and they could not be happier, wishing they had done it sooner.

Let's talk about the four steps in a little more detail...

⚙ Step 1: Good Oral Hygiene

You've heard it before and have probably been hearing it since you were a child "Brush and floss your teeth." This recommendation is not just to prevent bad breath or remove food that is stuck between your teeth. Although those are both excellent reasons to comply, there is also a more serious reason to keep your toothbrush and floss nearby.

Recent studies have shown a direct link between gum disease and systemic disease. What happens in your mouth is directly related to the rest of your body. A good example of this is diabetes. Ninety-five percent of US adults with diabetes have gum disease with one-third of that group having advanced gum disease that has led to tooth loss. High blood sugar levels lead to increased bleeding and inflammation of the gums. By improving your oral hygiene, you can decrease your A1c numbers and your risk of other chronic diseases such as cancer or heart disease.

Being an entrepreneur, you must remain healthy. Brushing and flossing will not only give you fresh breath when speaking to that new prospect, it can also keep you healthy and running at your best.

My recommendations: Brush twice a day, once in the morning and once before you go to bed. Floss at least once a day. A powered toothbrush is more effective than a manual toothbrush. Always choose a soft bristle toothbrush.

⚙ Step 2: Good Alignment

Are your teeth crooked? Do you have spaces between your teeth? Are your teeth crowded? Crooked teeth, crowding, and spaces are all complaints of patients who are not happy with their smile. These factors are important to your appearance and the success of your business. They can also affect your ability to eat and your hygiene.

Not being able to chew your food properly because of spaces or missing teeth can lead to gastrointestinal problems such as acid reflux or IBS. Crowding or crooked teeth make it difficult to brush and floss properly leaving areas of plaque on the teeth and food debris between the teeth. Both conditions can cause inflammation and bleeding of the gums as well as bad breath.

Crooked teeth, crowding, or spacing are all conditions that can be fixed easily. There are various dental treatments available to you such as Invisalign or braces, veneers, implants, or crowns. One of the solutions for crooked or crowded teeth is braces also called orthodontic treatment. When most people think of braces, they think of the old school metal brackets or "train tracks."

Metal brackets are still available, but with the advancements in dentistry, we have a new way of straightening teeth with clear aligners. Invisalign is a popular brand of clear aligners. With this treatment, there are no brackets or metal. Instead, clear trays are worn twenty to twenty-two hours a day. The trays are changed every two weeks and most cases can be completed in six months or less. My patients love the invisible look of the aligners and are happy with the results.

If you are not interested in braces but still want a great smile, veneers or crowns may be an option for you. Veneers are thin wafers of porcelain that is permanently bonded to the front of your tooth. It is a great option and a quick way to achieve a beautiful white smile. Crowns are like veneers but cover the front and the back of your tooth. Some of the reasons why you may need a crown versus a veneer include an existing crown on your tooth, a chipped or fractured tooth, or a discolored tooth. All these things will be considered by your dental professional when determining which treatment is best for you.

A great treatment option for missing teeth or spaces is implants. An implant is a metal post which is surgically placed into your jaw bone and restored with a crown. Implants can be used to restore a single missing tooth or multiple teeth. It is also a great option to stabilize dentures, allowing patients to feel more secure with their dentures and giving them more food options.

As an entrepreneur, your appearance is so important. How you show up will determine whether a client chooses to work with you or buy your product which ultimately affects your bottom line. Loving your smile will give you the confidence to go after that next big client or take the risk to start your own business.

My recommendations: Invest in your smile. An investment in your smile is an investment in your success.

⚙ Step 3: Good Dentist

Most adults have some anxiety about going to the dentist. However, you don't have to dread your dental appointments. With some research and insight, you can easily find a good dentist who can make the experience positive and rewarding for you. The relationship that you develop with your dentist can have a profound effect on your oral hygiene, your overall health, and your career. Here are a few qualities of a good dentist:

- Seeks to educate you about your dental needs
- Answers any questions you may have
- Takes the time to listen to your concerns and past experiences

- Includes you in all decisions regarding your dental treatment

- Informs you about your oral condition and recommendations before performing any dental treatment

- Makes you feel comfortable in the dental chair

- Has a gentle touch

- Stops treatment when you ask them to

- Fully respects your decision regarding your dental treatment

- The staff is friendly and helpful

The standard recommendation is to visit the dentist twice a year for an exam, x-rays, and a cleaning. The reason for this recommendation is early prevention. Seeing the dentist twice a year allows problems to be detected early before they develop into larger dental issues costing you more time and money.

As an entrepreneur, time and money are valuable assets. There are more productive ways to spend your time and money than in the dental chair. Prevention is key!

My recommendations: Find a good dentist. See them twice a year, so you can stay at the top of your game.

⚙ Step 4: Good Treatment Plan

If you need major dental work, it's okay. You should not feel ashamed or embarrassed. You deserve a high five just for acting and making it to the appointment. Kudos to you!

Now that you are aware of your dental problems, a detailed treatment plan can be created for you. A treatment plan is a written approach to tackle your dental needs. It includes the services and procedures recommended by the dentist, fees for each procedure, and any insurance reimbursements. It is organized in a sequential order of most to least importance. You will usually review this written plan with the treatment coordinator. This is a great time to ask any financial questions you may have and structure the treatment plan to meet your budget and schedule needs. The plan will help you to take a step-by-step approach to resolve your dental problems.

It is a common belief that dental treatment is expensive. A good treatment plan can make your dental treatment more affordable by breaking it down into several appointments allowing you to pay as you go. There are other payment options available to you such as financing, medical credit cards, and loans.

No dental insurance? No problem. Many entrepreneurs do not have dental insurance, but this is no reason to neglect your dental health. Many dental offices offer dental savings plans or can help you select a private insurance or discount plan.

My recommendations: Tackle your dental fear. Create a plan to take care of your dental treatment.

Successful entrepreneurs understand the importance of their appearance and how it can affect the success of their business. Being able to smile with confidence is priceless and a key component of your appearance. Losing the guilt, shame, and fear associated with dental treatment is easy with the Priceless Smile Formula. Contact me at www.drkimberlydds.com for your COMPLIMENTARY Smile Analysis. Together we can discuss your problems, your options and create your transformation!

YOUR INNATE SUPER POWERS FORMULA

Dr. M. Samm Pryce

Learn your five innate superpowers to take charge of your health naturally. This chapter will teach you how to prevent illness and maximize health.

I have always wanted to be a doctor! It started in the third or fourth grade when I did a report on the heart. I fell in love. From that moment forward, I knew that I wanted to become a cardiac surgeon. I wanted to heal the hearts of the world, and most importantly, I wanted to work on the inside and see all the intricacies that I learned about while researching for my report.

I worked very hard throughout elementary and high school. I was in the National Honor Society and a member of LOTS of clubs, including Jack and Jill of America- Atlanta Chapter. I accepted a Howard Hughes Biomedical Honors Scholarship to Xavier University in New Orleans, LA. They were, at the time and still are, number one in placing minorities in medical school. So, I was well on my way to fulfilling my dream of becoming a cardiac surgeon.

During college, I worked a lot and maintained my scholarship. My junior year, however, I became deathly ill. I missed a week of school and work, and this was so out of character that my friends dragged me to the hospital. I was misdiagnosed and spent the next week in my apartment vomiting and so tired that I didn't even want to take a shower. My aunt came over and rushed me back to the hospital where I was diagnosed with a self-limiting disease (it must clear itself). I went to see the specialist hoping that I could just take a pill, do surgery, or something, so I could get back to school. Your junior year before med school is super important, and I was already well into the process of applying to medical school. I did not need to miss any more school. The specialist dropped the bomb that there was NOTHING that they could do AND it would take months for me to heal.

I went home with my aunt and was quarantined. I read the book that my mom had sent about natural therapies and tried some. I felt better in a week and begged to go back to the specialist to see if I could get clearance to go back to school. The doctor did indeed clear me but would not acknowledge that my speedy recovery was due to the natural therapies that I applied.

I healed myself with natural therapies in record time! This made me start thinking about another way of doing medicine, so I started researching and found naturopathic medicine. I found that there are doctors who use evidence-based natural products (vitamins, minerals, food, etc.) to heal their patients. I also found that there are schools that teach this way of healing and that they are REAL LICENSED DOCTORS.

This near-death experience changed my life and is the reason I became a licensed naturopathic physician.

YOUR INNATE SUPER POWERS FORMULA

As a young girl, we all wanted to have some type of supernatural power, like the cartoon characters on the TV on Saturday mornings. In naturopathic medicine, we have six principles that we use to guide our daily practice, intentions, and decisions for our patients. One of the most important principles that makes us stand in a lane of our own is Vis Medicatrix Naturae: the healing power of nature.

The human body possesses the inherent ability to restore health. The naturopathic physician's role is to facilitate this process with the aid of natural, nontoxic therapies.

*Your body in its infinite wisdom, created by God, can heal itself when given the proper tools to stimulate the healing process.

I will teach you five ways to increase this innate power within. They are the ones that I have identified as the *most important* ones. Each of the five is independent of each other and can work alone to increase your powers, but when used together, they create a synergy. I call these five the SUPER POWERS. Here are the five that you need to master to be the superhero that I know you can be:

⚙ #1: Sleep

One of the three things that I ask patients about extensively is their sleeping pattern.

Not getting the proper amount of sleep or the proper type of sleep can be just as detrimental to your health as constantly eating processed/junk foods. When you get the sleep that you need, your body naturally makes a hormone called melatonin. This is the master hormone of our immune system, thus making it is a bonus while we sleep. I developed a system to help my patients called the N.A.P.P.™ System. Let me introduce you to my way of ensuring successful sleeping.

Say NO.

1. Say no to caffeine after 4 p.m. (could be 12 p.m. for you).

2. Say no to blue lights at least one hour before bedtime. These are lights that affect sleeping

and relaxation that are emitted from screens (TV, laptop, phone, and tablets).

3. Say no to clutter under your bed.

4. Say no to electronics near the head of the bed.

5. Say no to bringing work home.

Appropriate sleep and amounts of sleep matter.

1. You should be asleep from 10 p.m. to 2 a.m. at minimum to allow your body to make natural melatonin. This is the master hormone of the immune system.

2. You need more than six hours of sleep nightly. Some need more. Take three nights consecutively and record what time you go to sleep and what time you naturally wake up without an alarm clock. Average this, and this is the amount of sleep that you need.

Plan a bedtime routine and do the same thing each night.

1. Drink a cup of warm tea.

2. Take a relaxing bath or shower.

3. Read or journal.

Always end the night with a positive thought.

1. Get a jar and place at least one positive thing that happened in the jar at night.

2. Get a journal and write at least one positive thing that happened that day.

⚙ #2: Hydration

Our bodies are made up of more than 60 percent water, so obviously this is very important for our health. Drinking half your weight in ounces of water daily (not just eight glasses, but that is a good start) can act as a medicine and anti-aging secret. The main reasons why water is so important:

1. Lubricates our joints to help us move pain free

2. Controls body temperature through sweating

3. Provides structural firmness to our cells and helps to make up blood, lymph, and waste (gastric secretions and urine). Which brings me to . . .

⚙ #3: Detox

This is the third and maybe the most important of the superpowers. Are you shitting properly and regularly? Poop is POWERFUL!

Do you realize that you are supposed to have a bowel movement after each meal that you eat? This physically rids your body of the toxins that have built up inside of you. It should not sit around festering for days. YUCK!

Here are some types of detox.

1. Physical:

- Cleansing using natural substances (water, foods/diet, teas, etc.) and can last days to weeks

- Colonic - Physically pulling the poop out of you

- Sweating - This can be achieved with physical activity (exercise, dancing, sex, etc.) or an infrared sauna

2. Emotional: This rids you of negative feelings

- Media - Both social and news outlets

- Friends and family

⚙ #4: Mindfulness

Our thoughts often dictate our actions, which in turn can be helpful or harmful to our health.

There are three practices that can increase your powers in this area if you practice them daily:

1. **Prayer** - Essential. It doesn't need to be out loud, long, or eloquent.

2. **Affirmations** - Mahatma Gandhi said, "A man is but the product of his thought. What he thinks, he becomes."

3. **Gratitude** - I have a jar and each night before bed I write at LEAST one thing from the day that I am grateful for. I open the jar on 12/31 or 1/1 and see all my blessings. Stay in the moment. It takes less muscles to smile than to frown.

⚙ #5: Diet

> *"Let food be thy medicine and
> medicine be thy food"*
> *– Hippocrates (Father of Medicine)*

You are literally what you eat. If you eat healthy, then...

What diet is the best? The one that you will stick to and that works for you.

I customize diets for my patients based on their genetics, and one of the markers that I use is blood typing. Your blood cells and food both contain lectins (a protein) and they fit together like a lock and key. Science has shown us (just like all keys do not work in the same lock) that not all foods are appropriate for everyone based on their blood type.

Here is a brief overview of blood type diet characteristics and why it is a superpower to boost your immunity:

1. Blood Type O: (The Hunter - strong, self-reliant, leader)

Medical Risks: Blood clotting disorders, inflammatory disease - arthritis, low thyroid production, ulcers, allergies

Diet Profile:

High Protein: Meat eaters

Meat, fish, vegetables, fruits

Limited: Grains, beans, legumes

Weight Loss Key:

AVOID

Wheat, corn, kidney beans, navy beans, lentil, cabbage, Brussels sprouts, cauliflower, mustard greens

AIDS

Kelp, seafood, salt, liver, red meat, kale, spinach, broccoli

2. Blood Type A: (The Cultivator- settled, cooperative, orderly, artistic visionary)

Medical Risks: Heart disease, cancer, anemia, liver/gallbladder disorders, Type 1 diabetes

Diet Profile:

Vegetarian

Vegetables, tofu, seafood, grains, beans, legumes, fruits

Weight Loss Key:

AVOID

Meat, dairy, kidney beans, lima beans, wheat

AIDS

Vegetable oils, soy foods, pineapple

3. Blood Type B: (The Nomad- balanced, flexible, creative)

Medical Risks: Type 1 diabetes, chronic fatigue syndrome, auto-immune disorders (lupus, ALS, MS)

Diet Profile:

Balanced Omnivore

Meat - **(NO chicken)**

Dairy, grains, beans, legumes, vegetables, fruits

Weight Loss Key:

AVOID

Corn, lentils, peanuts, sesame seeds, buckwheat, wheat

AIDS

Greens, eggs, venison, liver, licorice, tea

4. Blood Type AB: (The Enigma - rare, charismatic, mysterious)

Medical Risks: Heart disease, cancer, anemia

Diet Profile:

Mixed diet in moderation

Meat, seafood, dairy, tofu, beans, legumes, grains, vegetables, fruits

Weight Loss Key:

AVOID

Red meat, kidney beans, lima beans, seeds, corn, buckwheat

AIDS

Tofu, seafood, dairy, greens, kelp, pineapple

I hope that this has been helpful and that you will start applying one or all so that you too can be a superhero!

To become a part of my online community, you can go to https://www.facebook.com/groups/ TheVitalForce/

THE PROFIT FIRST FORMULA

Angela Randolph

I began feeling the financial squeeze in early 2015. I'd recently purchased a house on the other side of town to reduce my commute time, but I had no idea the area was considered a premium location. I couldn't wrap my head around the higher price point for the same house I had recently sold. But I had no time to ponder or debate the merits of the builder's pricing because the housing market was booming, and there were other buyers ready sign on the dotted line.

Just when I'd finally accepted the fact that my mortgage note was what it was, my transmission went out in my ten-year-old SUV. With a new vehicle, I had a car note to add to my already thinning budget. It was just one financial setback after the other, and for the first time ever in my adult life, I was experiencing financial duress. I was basically working to pay bills and was held hostage in the house I had grown to resent. After years of spending at will, I knew I needed to do something different to climb out of this hole and achieve the financial goals I'd had for my future.

I knew for sure that commerce was happening all around me. I just needed to get in the game in order to change my financial trajectory. So, in the summer of 2017, I officially launched my business. I had to take ownership of my past financial missteps and begin creating the life I truly wanted; that meant a journey of entrepreneurship. I wanted financial independence, security, and flexibility, and I knew I had to change the way I did things. It all started with a dramatic mindset shift. To expedite my exit from the nine to five, I hired a business coach who focused on scaling to a million-dollar business and a branding coach to catapult my brand with visuals to attract top notch clients and additional income opportunities. With this tried and true formula I've used in my own business, you, too, can achieve your financial goals and leave a legacy for your family.

Here are the five critical steps to accelerated growth:

THE PROFIT PRICE FORMULA

⚙ I. Price for Profit

Overwhelmingly, the women entrepreneurs who I've worked with in some capacity have all underpriced their goods and services. It's very important to have a pricing strategy in place for your business, especially when you are growing and scaling your operations.

Value Pricing

Create a value or unique selling proposition for your goods and services, outlining why your target audience should buy from you and why what you have to offer is more compelling than the competition. Next, you want to define and communicate the transformation your audience will receive when they engage with your products and services. Research your ideal customer's pains or problems that need to be solved. Become a sought-out expert in your field offering nuggets of value to your target audience. Once you have uniquely positioned yourself in the marketplace delivering on your promises, you can then demand a premium on your goods and services. Don't worry about excessive pricing; the market will determine this for you.

Pricing Options

Create varying versions of your offerings or bundle them with at least two to three price points for your customers to choose from. This gives your customers the ability to select the appropriate level for their budget, and as they scale and grow, they can engage at higher price points with your business in the future.

Profit First

It's important to know your profit target number upfront when developing your pricing strategy. Charging lower prices just to get a higher volume of customers is not a viable strategy, and it can lower the perceived value of your goods and services in the marketplace. Don't fall into the trap of pricing your offer just above costs to beat out the competition. You cannot grow or scale this way. Sure, it's okay to know how your business measures compared to the competition, but that shouldn't be the focal point of your pricing strategy.

⚙ II. Plan to Scale

Successful growth depends on a scalable business model that will increase profits over time. You don't want both your revenues and expenses to grow at the same rate because you'll likely generate a net loss or at best break even. Does your current business model allow you to scale your operations? Scaling your business will take planning, capital, systems, adequate staff, technology, and strategic partners.

Strategic Plan

The first step in developing your strategic plan is assessing where you are financially in your business. Noting the starting point allows you to measure your progress over time. If you want to double or triple sales, then what actionable steps are required in order to achieve this goal? What people, processes, systems, or technology must be in place in order to facilitate this growth? Create a measurable action plan outlining the steps that must be taken to achieve these specific goals. Monitor your plan with benchmarks, checkpoints, and milestones, making any necessary adjustments along the way.

Capital

How will you fund your growing operations? Will you borrow from a traditional bank through the SBA, or will you seek alternative sources of financing like online lending, peer-to-peer lending, crowdfunding, invoice financing, or investor capital? Assess all viable options that are suitable for your situation. Unless you have established business credit, you'll need to personally guarantee any financing, so it's important to know your credit score and clean up any errors on your credit report.

Systems

Developing processes and procedures for your operations is key to scaling your business. You also want to design these processes to be repeatable in delivering your products and services to clients. Creating a new customized process for each customer will hamper your efforts to grow and scale your business. When you have documented teachable processes, you can measure the effectiveness of those processes and tweak any that need improvement. Quality control is easily monitored when you use systems to deliver goods and services to your clients.

Technology

If you haven't already, it's time to embrace technology. There are so many applications and software tools out there to assist small business owners in every facet of their company. Anything from project management tools, CRMs, inventory tracking, human resources, accounting software, mobile invoicing, etc. Using technology to run your business more efficiently and effectively saves time and money as you scale your operations.

⚙ III. Upgrade your Marketing Strategy

If you want to grow your business, then you must upgrade and execute a strategic marketing plan.

Relying solely on referrals won't get you to a seven-figure business at an accelerated pace. You'll need to increase your sales volume, which involves optimizing exposure to your target audience via marketing and promotion strategies. Having a lead generation system and tools to track and follow up on those leads is critical in your marketing strategy. Really hone in on where your ideal customers are and how to reach them. There are several marketing and advertising channels you can explore that's appropriate for your target audience.

As you develop your marketing plan, be sure to address the following items:

- What is your specific growth and sales goals?

- What resources will you use for marketing and how you will use them?

- What is the appropriate marketing budget for your goals?

- How will you engage, attract, and generate leads (email marketing, social media, TV, radio, print media, video, influencer, content marketing, and/or public relations, etc.)?

- How will you measure the success of your marketing plan?

Invest in good marketing tools and automate as much of the process as you can. Outsource tasks such as video editing and other specialized functions to save time and team resources.

⚙ IV. Build a Winning Team

Having a capable and results-oriented team is a must in growing your business to seven figures. You want a team that can handle a high level of activity as well as share in your core values and mission as a business.

Delegation

Be sure to define the roles needed for your organization. Also, have job descriptions and standard operating procedures documented and in place prior to hiring. Get comfortable with delegating tasks to your team because you cannot grow and scale your business doing everything yourself. You also don't want to undermine the process with extreme micromanagement of team members.

Hiring/Firing

Hiring mistakes can cost you money and setbacks in your business, so this process should be done carefully and methodically when considering candidates. Have a pool of candidates to select from for specific positions. Conduct in-depth interviews to see if the candidate is qualified for the position and a culture fit for the company. You also want to hire people who work well in collaborative teams. If you are hiring independent contractors, make sure your service agreements are solid and reviewed by an attorney to protect the interests of the business. On the flip side, if things are not working out as you envisioned and after a documented warning process, don't procrastinate with removing poor performing team members. Also, be sure to follow your local and state employment laws. It's very important to have the right people on board because it's crucial to the success of the business.

Compensation & Incentives

Competitive salaries and performance incentives increase retention and keeps team members motivated and engaged. Employees and independent contractors are handled differently in terms of pay structures and management of daily tasks. Develop a performance evaluation process that rewards your team for accomplishing goals set in advance and align them with overall company performance. Besides money, reward systems can include praise or recognition such as "employee of the month" or paid time off. With adequate reward systems, team members will be invested in the success of the company and level up their individual performance.

⚙ V. Get A CFO

As you level up your business, it's imperative that you have a Chief Financial Officer (CFO) as part of your C-Suite leadership team to help guide your growth. The stakes are much higher at the growth phase of your business with a team depending on you to make payroll and customers relying on you to deliver quality goods and services. You also owe it to yourself to invest in resources that will elevate your business, so you are better equipped to achieve your financial goals. Hire a dedicated expert to handle all things financial for your business such as the accounting, budgeting, payroll, cash flow, tax compliance, state and federal audits, strategic planning, forecasting, financing, risk management, etc.

CFOs are responsible for protecting the assets and interests of the business and mitigating your risks and reducing your liabilities. It's not an area you can afford to overlook or put on the back burner. The CFO also analyzes all things that impact your profits and works with you on a financial plan to improve your bottom line. CFOs are a critical part of your team that will allow you, the CEO, the time and resources you need to focus on operations. Having access to the expertise of a finance professional is an invaluable asset to your business in the growth stage and beyond.

If all this seems overwhelming, just know you are not alone; I'm here to help.

Join my online community of entrepreneurs who all have similar goals of growing and scaling their business to seven figures at https://www.facebook.com/groups/MoneyMetricsWE/

Also, to get a free E-Book *5 Ways to Improve Cash Flow*, visit www.angelarandolph.com

THE CUSTOMER CHEMISTRY FORMULA

Terri D. Sanders

In 1978, I graduated from college with a degree in journalism/ public relations. At that time when I took a marketing class, you purchased a large artist pad of paper and a set of art markers and you began graphic design. Our assignment was taking your initials and forming a logo. At that time the internet was not the staple that it is now.

I have been a serial entrepreneur for over thirty-five years. My businesses have included being a seamstress, wedding planner, baker, Certified Balloon Artist (CBA) (yes, there is a certification in balloon design), gift basketry, caterer, personal chef, and executive assistant. Yes, I have been busy. All my internet experiences were self-taught and through web courses. My businesses were real, but I never had true clarity on who I was serving and why. I used my God-given talents as my business base and worked hard with no real profit to show.

In 2016, my world began to shift, and my life was never going to be the same. I was diagnosed with breast cancer, my mother died, my best friend for over forty years had a fatal heart attack, and my husband of thirty-seven years had a massive stroke and died. In less than seven months, my life, my routine, and my support system changed.

We raised three children who are now adults and successful in their own lives: a contractor, a hospitality manager, and a CNN political commentator. At this point in my life, it was no longer about family, but it was all about ME. What was I going to do, and what was I leaving as my legacy?

In 2017, I decided that I wanted to have clarity and make my entrepreneurial goals sustainable in the marketplace. I was ready for a transformation. In 2018, I began with entrepreneurial coaching to get a clear perspective of what was a sustainable entrepreneurship model. I knew what an entrepreneur was, why I was an entrepreneur, and all about my product, but I had not mastered the how of sustainable business legacy. For nine months, I studied and was mentored. I had experienced the "expensive" hobby of entrepreneurship; now I was looking through a different lens to my future. I was ready for branding and connected with Jai Stone to bring me to the track I needed to run on to get to the success of the finish line. I strongly suggest that you invest in YOU, the most important company you will own.

I have been where you are, and I would like to share what was transformational for me through the development of the Customer Chemistry Formula that if applied to your entrepreneurial pursuits will richly benefit your business. I have over thirty-five years of being where you are, and I want to share with you the benefits of my experience and boots-on-the-ground knowledge to transform your business. Life is about strategies and processes, and I have learned that without these two elements you will continue a journey with no destination.

THE CUSTOMER CHEMISTRY FORMULA

There are five steps to the formula that transformed my life and is propelling my legacy. Whether you have a storefront, an online business, or are a solopreneur, this formula can be used to transform your business. People buy from those that they know, like, and trust. This formula will be a guideline to establishing a relationship with your customer that will establish you as the go-to business that can meet their needs. People do not always buy based on price. It is the relationship that is established that has the most influence. As you strategize for success, ask questions, and the answers will move you to the next level.

⚙ Step 1: Message

The Audience

If people buy from those that they know, like and trust, then your message is how the customer will get to know you, develop a liking to you, and trust that your product will meet their needs. Everyone is *not* YOUR customer. What your business offers is unique. There are particular people who your offering is designed for. Get to know *WHO* you are targeting with the message.

- Who is your target audience?

- How do you reach the audience you are marketing to?

Your What

- What are you offering to your customer?
- Services: personal or professional?

- Products: business-to-client or business-to-business?

- Is your offering unique in the marketplace?

The Information

Is your message being communicated clearly? If you presented it to an eight-year-old, could they tell you what you are offering? Keep it simple. Industry terms and specialty language will not get YOUR customer's attention.

The Experience

Part of your message is the experience that you offer to your customer. Customers are not just waiting to be sold with money in hand. Customers want to be "courted."

- How do you communicate to all your customer's senses?

- What colors are you using?

- If you are a brick and mortar store, what sound do they hear when they enter your shop?

- Is there a scent in your store?

- Is your merchandise touchable? Can the customer conveniently touch and try on items?

⚙ Step 2: Marketing

Everything you do circles back to the client you are serving. Knowing who your customer is also

5

means knowing WHERE your customer is and WHAT your customer is doing. Marketing is creating knowledge. The knowledge is brand awareness which is about putting your brand into the marketplace to be noticed. Your marketing should strive to be different. Your marketing is about the customer, not about YOU. The uniqueness of your offer and the value that it brings is demonstrated through marketing the product.

Some of the ways to get the word out about your product:

- Videos (Seven to ten buyers like to see videos about a product and its features.)
- Social Media: Facebook, Twitter, Snap Chat, LinkedIn, Instagram
- Postcards/flyers
- Emailing information
- Newsletters
- Newspaper advertising
- Broadcasting
- Mailers
- Interest articles about your product
- Testimonials from satisfied customers

Know Your Numbers

To know if your marketing is creating awareness; you should know your numbers. Know how many persons are getting your message. Technology gives us many ways to share information. The entrepreneur must stay current on technology trends. You must know where your customers are and how your information is being received. Demographics tells who your followers are by:

- Age
- Location
- Sex

Analytics provides an analysis of your customers actions:

- When they are looking at your information
- How long persons are looking at your information
- Specifically, how many people viewed the post
- Looking at your numbers gives you insight into what is working and what is not. Your analytics should be reviewed on a weekly basis. Depending on the numbers, you may want to pivot the information that you are supplying.

⚙ Step 3: Content

Your content should fit your brand. The information that you present should have value. Value should be targeted to your ideal client and what appeals to them. What information will best serve your audience and steer them to what you offer? Content is not only about selling, it is also about information. As the content creator, you must be providing relevant information styled to fit your brand. You must read and research to provide the latest trends information. Your content should be information that people are seeking. Educating with your content provides value to your reader.

Engaging people builds trust and lets the customer know you are looking for a relationship. In your content, ask questions. When you ask questions, people are more likely to be engaged. You should also be authentic. Be real with your audience. People relate to those who they believe are real. Remember, people do business with those that they know, like, and trust.

Consistency in distributing information on a regular basis is equally critical. If social media is being used, then daily or multiple postings per day provides content that customers can find and look forward to. If you are only present once per week or randomly, then you will not be top of mind when something that you provide is needed.

Examples of content:

- Videos
- Free product offers
- Tips/techniques
- Motivational quotes
- Podcasts
- Blogs
- Articles
- Emailing

⚙ Step 4: Conversion

Marketing is providing information. Through marketing, you want to move customers to buy. Buying is converting the client to a paid customer. Marketing and sales are connected because your product has value, and you deserve to be paid for it. Focus on how your product or service benefits the customer and how it will impact their lives. Conversion will happen when the customer sees that your product and your service is what they are looking for to answer their need. When your marketing actions position you as the leading authority in the marketplace, then conversion to customer will be a natural flow of revenues.

⚙ Step 5: Community/Culture

Once a customer is in your community of buyers, you should keep them coming back. Cultivating this loyalty requires that you remain in contact with them. Remember why the customer is your customer and keep that position of being their go-to for solutions through the content that you provide, the marketing strategies you employ, and by treating them "special." If you have employees, they are a part of your community also.

Customers

What are some of the things that you can do to keep customers in your community?

- Loyalty cards
- VIP Customer Designation
- Special discount included with a purchase to be used on next visit
- Name key customers as Influencers
- Feature customers in your communications as style makers (fashion)
- Send specific emails to customers on the email list
- Develop exclusivity for customers and honor it

Whatever is special treatment, treat the community that way.

Employees

Your employees are KEY members of your community. Employees are the persons who interact with your customers on a personal level. Treat your employees kindly. Have sale incentives. Offer rewards for accomplishments (e.g. an electronic device if sales numbers hit a goal or employee discounts on merchandise). Employees are part of your culture.

THE MONETIZE YOUR MINISTRY FORMULA

Arlecia "Dr. Lecia" Simmons, PhD, MDiv

In a world where social media allows us to curate our lives in ways that aren't reflective of reality, there are still a few places where authenticity rises above the noise and rhetoric.

In Christian churches, one never knows what might be done or spoken when the Holy Spirit is at work.

"Somebody better tell God thank you! If you think back over your life, you may recall a time when you could have died. I should have been dead, people. Years ago, I was driving home from a booty call, and I closed my eyes and I almost died." With tears flowing down my face and hands waving, I actually stood in front of hundreds of congregants and testified about how after a night of having sex outside of marriage God blocked me from crashing my car.

I mean telling a congregation on a Sunday morning that you almost died in a car accident after a booty call is just not how we envision overcoming by our testimonies. But on that morning as I transitioned the service from praise and worship to welcoming the visitors, I spoke a truth that had been hidden way down inside as I looked the part of being saved and sanctified. Like many who grew up in church, I loved Jesus but had made decisions that were my well-kept secrets. Later in that day after I surfaced outside of the holies of holies, I felt somewhat embarrassed until a sister at the church pulled me aside and thanked me for my transparency. "People don't know where God has brought us from," she said.

In that moment, I was reminded that even when our stories aren't sanitized and all aligned with the perfection of a Proverbs 31 woman, God will use our words to heal, restore hope, and uplift those who are hearers. How will those who need a word of hope, love, and even conviction get it if we refuse to speak because we're too ashamed of what the people will say? How will those in darkness find light if the light continues to hide in a corner and never reach its intended recipient?

As a marketplace marketing consultant, author, and speaker, I help those in church ministry reach people where they are, beyond the walls. Additionally, I help women in ministry and those discerning their calls identify and expand ministries through publishing, social media, and speaking using their authentic voices.

While God certainly uses social media for the expansion of the Gospel, the saturation of digital altars is intimidating to those who haven't embraced the technology and are still working out their own calls in fear and trembling. Some may say: "I don't have any followers?" or "I don't know what to say," or "I'm not comfortable in front of a camera." All of these excuses are similar to those the biblical prophets gave God when assigned specific tasks. Well, there are still no legitimate excuses—especially when professionals like me are here. People learn how to develop not only their authentic voice but also how to use technology to spread the Gospel.

Even after the many affirmations received throughout the years, it took years for me to embrace that God was calling me to service in a way that I had never envisioned for my life. Well, not quite. I had sensed that God was calling me to something greater than myself, but without a safe space to help me hear what the still small voice was saying, I muted it until I was no longer in control of the volume. In the final months of completing my Doctor of Philosophy degree at the University of Iowa, I finally surrendered to that voice that was ushering me into a space where I long believed women were not truly welcomed. I had seen women operate as evangelists, missionaries, and ordained ministers, yet I had little direct contact with women loosed from the shackles of discouragement of naysayers.

After answering one's call to ministry, it could take months, years, or even decades to finally discern the next steps to walk fully in your call. Having answered my call to ministry in my mid-thirties after studying for my dissertation research, a female minister entering ministry at thirty-five-years-old years, I realized women could use more coaching and mentoring to become all that God had ordained them to be.

While traditional avenues will continue to have their own challenges, delays, and roadblocks, God is always doing a new thing. Through means such as digital media, women called to ministry no longer must wait for the next opportunity to preach (which could take years).

THE MONETIZE YOUR MINISTRY FORMULA

PUBLISHING

In early centuries, Caucasian American women were able to spread the Gospel via writing when they were not allowed to formally preach. For women of color, literacy and access to publishing were delayed but are now avenues of consideration.

As it is written in Habakkuk 2:2, women with a ministerial call can now write the vision and make it plain. Those who see the vision tweeted, illustrated in a graphic on Instagram, and heard via Livestream can run with it and begin on the way God is calling them.

Is there a book that you've already written, but no one has read it because it's still being held hostage inside of you? While you're waiting for the next speaking assignment or opportunity to share your ministry, how could your book already be helping to heal people even before you arrive?

In 2014, I released my first book *Diggin' For Treasure: Jewels of Hope When Pressure & Time Collide,* which is part spiritual autobiography and part devotional. After years of blogging and sharing inspirational posts on social media, my followers began to request that I compile all my posts and blog entries into one space. The publication of *Diggin'* resulted in invitations to conduct women's bible studies as well as facilitate a women's conference session with two hundred and fifty in attendance. From there, I began to develop a study that could be used by other group leaders. Because of my obedience to publish the book, God opened doors beyond what I could ask or think while building my social media engagement. As I connected with more pastors and church leaders via social media, my virtual network began expanding and people I had never met began acknowledging my ministerial gifts. Additionally, I've been able to connect with ministry leaders and lay leaders who have the ear of the pastor or who are in positions to suggest special Sunday speakers.

CONTENT MARKETING

Although social capital is still the most prominent means used when church leaders select speakers to minister to their flock, those who don't know you personally may also come to learn of your voice through word-of-mouth coupled with blogging and social media that allows you to expand your sphere of influence.

By writing blogs and posting content that is beyond churchy clichés, you can spread the Gospel in relevant ways that may connect with believers and nonbelievers. If your message is authentic and relatable, those in ministry leadership may take note. Because social media allows us to blend our personal and professional lives, it's important to recognize its power to promote as well as tarnish one's brand. You can't talk about Jesus on every other post then go live popping bottles. There's being authentic after you have the testimony, then there's being irresponsible and not honoring the call of God on your life.

SHARING YOUR VOICE

Beyond assisting individual ministers with taking their message beyond the four walls, I also help church leaders discern how they can expand beyond the walls by using appropriate social media channels to reach people where they are, which could be at work, on the way to a game, or chilling at the house. Our global society is even reflected in the church, as congregations such as Trinity Unity Church of Christ in Chicago acknowledge each Sunday various people from around the world who are live streaming their Sunday services. For example, there's a group in Australia who meets at night to watch the Chicago church's Sunday morning service.

Both pew research and pastors whose churches employ electronic giving report how more and more people are using links shared on social media, websites, and text-to-give applications to financially support their ministries. The technology isn't just being used by existing congregants but also by livestream viewers who connect with ministries via social media. While I was in graduate school in Iowa, I spent countless snowy Sunday mornings viewing church via stream. Those ministries that I began to adopt as my cyber places of worship often coupled their streaming with strategic social media. At least two of the congregations have since hired "digital pastors." Although not all congregations will be able to hire a digital pastor, both small and large congregations can develop plans on how to engage those who worship with them beyond the walls of the church.

When Jesus needed to effectively communicate with those who worked the land and the sea, he used the language they understood and talked about sowing, reaping, and casting nets. If we are to continue to grow the ministries God has called us to, it won't be through means that reached earlier generations. With our authentic voices, we must consider that the people we are called to won't always be gathered in a specific space at a specific time; they may be thousands of miles away in a remote location. But how will they hear, unless we power up our phones, tablets, and laptops and begin to share the words God has given us to say? How will those who need our words never hear them because we've allowed technology and new applications to defeat us?

THE DREAM TEAM SUCCESS FORMULA

Jamella Stroud

At the age of twenty-six, in 2009, I started my first traditional business as a seasonal tax preparer. My first year in business I operated solo, but I learned quickly if I wanted to scale and reach multiple six figures, I needed a team.

Before the second tax season, I sought out team members. Although I knew I needed a team to support my dream for the company, I didn't have a strategic hiring process. Like many entrepreneurs, I hired people I knew and people I'd previously worked with who had skills and qualities I needed to fulfill the dream. The second year, I hired two receptionists, two tax preparers, and an office manager who was the business rainmaker, apart from myself. I had no previous experience with team building besides watching my dad, who was a pharmaceutical sales representative, build a team (and he wasn't selling over-the-counter drugs). I was smart enough to know there were some things I had to have in place, so I hired a payroll company. I also knew each employee had to complete an application, and I needed to keep a record of it, but there was so much I was missing in the formula of creating a dream team.

Fast forward to my fourth season in business: we had two locations, about fifteen employees, and a multi six-figure business. To my dismay, I closed and bankrupted the business after achieving amazing success, but I learned a lot along the way. I've reinvented myself, learned from all the lessons and mistakes, and launched SURGE Coaching & Consulting.

There are two parts to building a DREAM TEAM. The first part is about you as the CEO. (And we'll discuss this part when we break down DREAM.) The second part is about the team. (We will discuss this part when we break down TEAM.) As the CEO, you hold the DREAM for your company. You received the dream; it belongs to you. You are responsible for your dream; therefore, it's in your best interest to hire people who will support you in fulfilling the dream. If your dream for your company can be fulfilled with you and you alone, you are playing small.

DREAM STATEMENT

Before you begin planning for a team, you must be clear on the dream of the company. I'm not suggesting you should have a formal business plan, but you should have a written plan that clearly states what your dream company looks like, including vivid details of the company, furniture, location, what it feels like, positions your company has for others, etc. I like to call it a Dream Statement. Once you have your dream statement for your company, you can then think about who you'll need to fulfill the dream.

THE DREAM TEAM SUCCESS FORMULA

D - DEVELOP ORGANIZATIONAL CHART

Once you have the written dream statement, you will develop your organizational chart. The organizational chart is an infographic that shows the structure of your company roles and the relationship and rank of each position. The organizational chart shows who each position reports to also. You, as the CEO, should always be at the top of your organizational chart, or if you choose to not function as the CEO of your company, that's fine too. However, the CEO's role should be at the top of the chart. Remember, this chart is specific to your business. It's created from your DREAM Statement, so it doesn't have to look like another company's organizational chart because your DREAM Statement may not be the same as another company's.

Once you have completed the organizational chart, you will begin to see what positions are most important according to your company growth and ability to fill positions. Some positions on your chart may be positions your company will grow into but still include them on your chart.

R - REFINE JOB DESCRIPTION

The organizational chart has been developed and completed. Now, you can begin refining your job descriptions. You will utilize the organizational chart to know which job description is most important to create. It's important that you create a job description for all positions on your chart, although there will be some that are more important than others. When creating the title, you can be creative; the position title doesn't matter as much as the other parts of the job description.

The job description is an internal, formal, legal document that describes in detail the tasks, responsibilities, technology skills, competence skills, work activities, physical demands, preferred education, and experience for the position. The job description is an essential part of building your DREAM TEAM; it holds the company and team member accountable for work performance. When the job description is not clear, team members become confused about their responsibilities and how to carry it out. The job description is a road map for you as the CEO and the employer, providing clarity on the daily tasks and responsibilities for the team members.

E - ESTABLISH ONBOARDING PROCESS

The job descriptions are refined and complete. You are almost ready for your team. Now, you must establish your onboarding process. The onboarding is the process of getting new team members adjusted to the social and performance aspects of their job. During this process, the new team member learns detailed and specific information about your company. There are three types of onboarding that new team members can potentially go through:

Passive Onboarding

Passive onboarding is informal and unorganized. It addresses compliance issues for new team members such as new hire paperwork, W-4 or I-9 forms, and benefits and payroll forms. It also includes some clarification where team member understands his or her role and expectations.

High Potential Onboarding

High potential onboarding is formal but somewhat unorganized. It addresses everything in passive onboarding and some culture aspects of the company. Addressing culture helps new hires understand company goals, values, and culture. They also learn company lingo. Example of learning company lingo and culture is MOE's Southwest Grill. Upon entering MOE's employees say, "Welcome to MOE's." This is something that was learned during onboarding.

Proactive Onboarding

Proactive onboarding is formal and organized, addressing everything in passive and high potential compliance, clarification, culture, and connection. This makes sure team members feel a part of and welcome in the company socially and according to performance by other team members and management.

You choose the onboarding process that works for your company. Just make sure it's the same process for every team member.

A - ADMINISTER INTERVIEWS AND HIRE

Now that you've established the onboarding process, job descriptions, and organizational chart, it's time to administer interviews, but wait! Let's not move too fast. You must establish questions and an interview style. There are two types of interview styles:

Structured

A structured interview is a uniform way of interviewing every applicant based on the specific job description. During the interview, the applicant is asked the same question according to the job applied for. You're probably wondering, "How do I know what questions to ask applicants?" Remember I told you the job description is important? Here's why. You will create interview questions for each job according to task, responsibilities, and skills required for position. You should have at least one question per task and responsibility.

Unstructured Interview

The unstructured interview is an interview that feels like a conversation. It's informal because there are no prearranged questions. There may be certain topics you cover that's related to the tasks, responsibilities, and skills, but the interview is open and flexible. Although you may offer unstructured interviews, it's wise to have specific areas you'll address. This style of interview creates an opportunity to get to know the applicant better.

You're ready to post the job announcement, interview, and hire. When posting job announcements, you are selling the job to potential applicants. The job description is not the job announcement although you will use things from the job descriptions to create announcements.

It's time to administer interviews and hire your team.

M - MODEL CULTURE AND VALUES

Your new hire should have gone through your onboarding process. Now, you can model the company culture and values before them. They are new to your company, so what you teach them through behavior is what they will duplicate. I've seen many CEOs upset with their team member's behavior only to find out they taught them the behavior. Be sure you hold true to your values.

The first ninety days is crucial to your team success. Below are some things you should do within the first week and first ninety days.

First Week

- Issue a copy of the job description, handbook, and non-disclosure.

- Complete orientation during onboarding.

- Have a manager discuss expectations and goal setting.

- Review processes, systems, and software.

Thirty to Ninety Days

- Training

- Allow job shadowing

- Ask for feedback
- Plan performance review

During the first ninety days, a foundation for team member success is to be laid. Be thorough. Everything in DREAM is CEO-focused. There are things you are responsible for before you build the team.

Now, you're ready to focus on the TEAM.

T - TRAIN THE TEAM

This is my favorite part of the DREAM TEAM formula. I love the people aspect of DREAM TEAM. There are stages to training the teams because the team is in a continuous state of training. Upon hiring, there is a stage of training for team members according to their job. Please note that all training should be directly related to job description.

Utilize the job descriptions to know what areas of training your company needs to offer. For example, a skill required for a particular position is active listening. Upon entering the company, the team member would receive training in this area. Later the team member may need advanced active listening training to master the skill. When additional or new training is needed, you can train the team or hire someone like SURGE Coaching & Consulting to come and train the team or send the team to off-site trainings (whether virtually or in person). Do not train your team in areas that you are not an expert in.

Training your team is key to your company's success; we at SURGE Coaching & Consulting believe people development increases performance. The more developed your team is the higher their performance and the greater the profits.

E - EVALUATE THEIR PERFORMANCE

To evaluate is to determine the significance or quality of work a team member has. The evaluation is about past performance of the team members. It's also a tool that can be used to provide feedback to create an opportunity for employee recognition.

There are steps to completing the evaluation process.

- Develop evaluation forms - The form should be fair, consistent, objective, and protect employee interests while focusing on essential tasks and responsibilities with different ranges for each to measure performance.

- Identify performance measures - Be sure to use standard performance measures. Examples: A receptionist task is data entry of client information into computer. Standard performance measures for task could be seven to twelve entries per day (quantity) with error rate of less than 3 percent (quality). However, standard performance measures don't work for subjective areas like attitude.

- Set guidelines for feedback - It's important to create opportunities for team members to give feedback about the company's performance. You want to also provide balanced feedback to the team, stating what they're good at and areas of opportunity. Also, outline expectations for improvement so that the team will know what's required to improve.

- Create a disciplinary and termination process - Use verbal warnings and written warnings before termination. When a team member has disciplinary issues, be sure to document date, time, issue, and goals and allow team members to sign. Make sure they are aware of the next steps if another incident happens.

- Create an evaluation schedule - Once you've built the evaluation process, decide when to conduct evaluations. I suggest the first evaluation happens after ninety days and then annually.

A - ACCESS THEIR POTENTIAL

It's important to complete the evaluation which focuses on the past performance of the team because it's a predictor of future performance.

When accessing team potential, it's all about predicting their future performance. The evaluation is the tool you'll use for this. You'll utilize this to determine if a team member qualifies for a promotion.

M - MONITOR THEIR GROWTH

Although there is an annual evaluation in place, don't rely on it alone. Monitoring team performance keeps them motivated and allows them to know how they are performing on a regular basis.

To monitor their growth, you can create feedback sessions, individually or collaboratively. Doing frequent monitoring allows the team to be aware of areas of opportunities for growth and recognition. You have the opportunity to frequently celebrate your team.

I've said a lot, and you're probably still trying to digest the D in DREAM TEAM formula. That's why I recommend you follow me for more details. Go to http://bit.ly/FollowCEOCoach

And to get a free copy of my first chapter of *SURGE the CEO Guide to Baggage Free Success*, visit bit.ly/SURGECEOBook

MEET THE AUTHORS

JAI STONE

Jai Stone is an award-winning master brand strategist and social media superhero with over 50,000 online followers. Her client list includes corporations such as the Coca-Cola Company, NASCAR, and Turner Broadcasting System, as well as several high-profile entrepreneurs.

Ms. Stone is a sought-after saucy speaker, courageous content creator, and three-time bestselling author. Her thought-provoking content and stories have been featured with Forbes, BET, Huffington Post, ESPN, Black Enterprise, and Essence Magazine.

As a highly-respected brand expert and one of the most respected voices online, Jai's insights and expertise has led to recognition by Who's Who of Black Atlanta, Young and Powerful for Obama and earning the coveted 'Best Marketing Firm in Atlanta' title from Atlanta Tribune Magazine. Among her proudest moments, Jai is most humbled to have been a featured contributor in The State of Black America Report from the National Urban League.

Learn more at http://jaistone.com/

SAM ALDRIDGE MOORE: SAM

SAM "The HR Savvy Pro" (Sam Aldridge Moore) has over twenty years of talent acquisition and human resources experience. She offers workforce training and consulting to organizations who have a desire to cultivate, manage, and grow a diverse workforce. SAM has an MBA, is an active member of the Society of Human Resources Management (SHRM), holds a certification in crucial conversations, and is a Lean Six Sigma – Green Belt.

Learn more at https://www.hrsavvypro.com

SHA' CANNON

Sha' Cannon positions entrepreneurs to propel their profit potential to create freedom in their businesses and regain control over their lives. She does this by helping increase their credibility, visibility, and bankability. She guides her clients to effectively write and publish a book as the quickest path to true credibility, raising visibility for themselves and their business through content, as well as increasing their profits with additional product and service offerings. Sha's clients are usually experts, coaches, and speakers who are serious about their entrepreneurship and would like to propel the profits in their businesses.

Learn more at www.ShaCannon.com
Sha' is on social media as @ExpertlySha

YOLANDA V. CORNELIUS

Yolanda V. (Yolanda Cornelius), The Make It Happen Coach, helps highly driven women shift their mindset to create sustainable action plans and change their lives thirty days at a time.

After investing nearly twenty years of her talents, education, and energy into her accounting career and entrepreneurial endeavors with only moderate success, she decided to revamp her life. She said goodbye to an unfulfilling, dead-end position, let go of self-imposed obligations to her family, and stopped settling for mediocre opportunities for success. She moved to a new city and self-published her first book on Amazon.com in 2017 titled *Fit, Fabulous and Focused: How to Create the Life You Want After Forty*.

Learn more at www.yolandav.com

DR. NII-DAAKO DARKO

Dr. Nii Darko is a board-certified general surgeon who is pushing the limits of the status quo. He hosts *Docs Outside the Box*, an Apple Podcast ranked Top 100 in Careers, where he highlights stories of doctors doing extraordinary things outside of medicine to inspire doctors to think outside the box. Dr. Nii Darko holds a Doctor of Osteopathic Medicine (DO) from Kansas City University and an MBA in Health Care Leadership from Rockhurst University. He completed his general surgery residency at Morehouse School of Medicine. He also completed a Trauma/Surgical Critical Care fellowship at the University of Miami.

Learn more at https://www.drniidarko.com/

CHRIS DAVIS

Chris serves as a strategic adviser for startup companies and is currently the Director of Education at Active Campaign. Providing him with exposure to all types of companies facing unique challenges to grow online. These experiences are what Chris uses to help make the process of adopting technology in your marketing easier to understand and implement. Chris also served as the Head of Marketing Automation for two years at a startup called Lead pages, where he built out the marketing system that helped raise $37 million of funding over three rounds.

Chris holds a bachelor's degree in electrical engineering from Kansas State University and an MBA with an emphasis on Project Management. With more than 12 years of professional experience in the technology and business space, he is passionate about helping companies grow strategically using technology in their marketing.

Learn more at https://automationbridge.com

DR. KIMBERLY HARPER

Dr. Kimberly Harper, DDS is a cosmetic and restorative dentist, speaker, and author. She helps her patients restore their smiles and regain their confidence so they can live, love, and laugh without embarrassment. Affectionately known by her patients and community as Dr. Kimberly, she's run a successful private practice in the Dallas area for nearly fifteen years.

As a respected professional in her field, she earned her doctorate from the University of Iowa College of Dentistry and holds a Master of Business Administration from Texas Tech University. She believes a smile is the most beautiful thing you can wear and wants everyone she encounters to love their smiles!

Learn more at http://drkimberlydds.com/

DR. M. SAMM PRYCE

As a world class expert in natural medicine, Dr. Samm is a licensed naturopathic physician. She is sought after for her mastery of the Blood Type Diet, epigenetics, and nutrigenomics. Through her concierge private medical practice, books, and retreats she helps to bridge conventional and alternative medicine to transform illness into wellness. As the Chief Medical Officer for Balanced Integration, PLLC, she listens, cares, and then guides her patients to better health using naturopathic medicine.

Learn more at https://www.drsammnd.com/

ANGELA RANDOLPH

Angela is a CPA with a BBA in accounting and finance and an MBA in finance and management. Angela's professional career spans over twenty years in accounting, finance, audit, and tax. Angela helps frustrated CEOs experiencing accelerated growth manage their in-house financial needs, so they can focus on their business and not their books. As the Founder and CEO of Stellar Ledgers LLC, Angela is very passionate about helping women entrepreneurs achieve their financial goals by providing outsourced CFO and Controller services, financial coaching, and consulting. Angela is a native of New Orleans, LA and is currently based in the greater Houston, TX area.

Connect with Angela at www.angelarandolph.com

TERRI D. SANDERS

Terri D. Sanders is a serial entrepreneur. In thirty-five years, she has been a seamstress, wedding planner, Certified Balloon Artist (CBA), caterer, personal chef, and bread baker extraordinaire, just to name a few.

In 2017, God changed Terri's circle, and she took that as a sign for her to turn the corner and follow her passion. Meeting and embracing Jai Stone was a real eye opener and *gamechangHER*.

Terri has been on a journey of clarity and expansion of her territory. She has since embraced the mantra: When you have a roadmap, the journey is easier. When you change your mindset, you change your outlook.

Learn more at https://tdsandersassociates.com/

ARLECIA "DR. LECIA" SIMMONS

Arlecia "Dr. Lecia" Simmons, PhD, MDiv, is an award-winning journalist who has taken her storytelling gifts from the pages of newspapers to the pulpit and now onto social media.

As a marketplace ministry consultant, Dr. Lecia helps ministry leaders reach people where they are. The Charleston, S.C. native is also a Gullah Geechee Ambassador who shares her culture through presentations and her Branducation Tees.

Her passion for writing and ministry has come together in a devotional book *Diggin' For Treasure: Jewels of Hope When Pressure & Time Collide*. Visit www.drlecia.com for more info about her work.

Learn more at http://drlecia.com/

JAMELLA STROUD

Jamella Stroud CEO, coach, and founder of Naked & Unafraid Movement is an international transformational speaker, author, and coach who values Jesus, family, community, and building relationships. After leaving her first career as a tax accountant to pursue her life's work, she launched her second business Surge Coaching & Consulting. She brings a sudden, strong burst of energy, creativity, new ideas, and thinking to each client interaction disturbing the norm and status quo, pushing boundaries within clients so they can thrive and be their best selves. Jamella has also spoken for and worked with universities and national organizations.

Learn more at http://www.jamellastroud.com/